Go! Stock! Go!

A Stock Market Guide for Enterprising Children
and their Curious Parents*

*Everything you were afraid your kids would ask

Written *by* **Bennett Zimmerman**
Richly Illustrated *by* **Kathy Kamel**

The FOURTH WAY WORLD, LLC
1318 Yale Street
Front Suite
Santa Monica, CA 90404

For information regarding special discounts for bulk purchases, or for affinity, personalized, or corporate branded versions please contact bennett@gostockgoinvest.com

Manufactured in the United States of America

Library of Congress Cataloging-in-Publication Data is available.

ISBN 978-0-9907890-1-7 (trade paperback)
ISBN 978-0-9907890-2-4 (mobi ebook)
ISBN 978-0-9907890-3-1 (epub ebook)
ISBN 978-1-5085155-0-0 (library edition)

Visit us at www.gostockgoinvest.com

For Kendra Johnson

Go! Stock! Go!

"Go baby, go baby, go!

"Go baby, go baby, go baby go," Harry Johnson yelled at his computer screen by the television in the den.

"Hey, Dad, the only baby I know is Harold, asleep in the next room," said Nathan, Harry's bright, young son. "Who are you talking to?"

"You see, Nathan, I bought stock in the **Future Is Now Internet Company**, and the price of its shares is going through the roof today.

We're making lots of money. Now I can buy you that bike you want, the car I want, and take the whole family back to Mega Beach Resorts over the summer. See what I mean?"

"Actually, Dad, other than the car, the bike, and a vacation at Mega Beach Resorts, I didn't understand a single thing you said. And my teacher told me I have good com-pre-hen-sion." Nathan shrugged his shoulders, ignoring this adult video game for now.

Fortunately, Sue, Nathan's mother, was listening from the doorway. "I think a better explanation is in order."

Sue was a teacher by training. More importantly, she was the President of the *Wall Street in Suburbia Investment Club*, a collection of friends who got together every week to plan investments in the stock market.

"Nathan, when Dad buys a **stock**," Mom said, "or anyone buys a stock, what they're actually buying is a piece of a company. That's why some people say they're buying **shares** in a company. A share, or a portion of that company, becomes their own property."

Nathan frowned. "Well, that sounds like an exciting way to waste my money—buying a piece of a company. What can I do with that?"

"Good question," Mom replied. "Companies do lots of things. They make products that people want, but what a company really wants to do at the end of the day is make money. It's like that time you started a lemonade stand or mowed lawns around the neighborhood. You did it to make money. A company is doing the same thing; it's trying to make money. When you own a share of that company, you have a right to some of the money, or a portion of the wealth, that the company is creating. You become a part owner of that company."

"I like the sound of that," Nathan said, grinning. "Nathan. Owner. Cool. I feel rich already."

"Actually," Mom continued, "you only become rich if your company makes money, or a profit, from its business. The company takes in money every time it sells something—that's called **revenue**. If its revenue is larger than its **costs**—that's the money it spends on materials, workers, buildings, or any other items—then it makes a **profit**. Every year that profit belongs to the owners, or **shareholders**, of the company."

"Okay, so did that internet company just pay Dad a lot of money?"

"No, not today anyway. When a company makes money, it can give back some of those profits to the shareholders as a **dividend**. It sends a check or makes a direct deposit to the owner's account, depending on how many shares each owner has in the company. Or, many companies put that money right back in the company so they can make even more money in the future. That's called **reinvesting**, and it's how small companies become big companies. As the company becomes bigger and richer, the **value** of your shares rises."

"Wait a minute," Nathan said. "If I remember correctly, my lemonade stand didn't exactly set the world on fire. Come to think of it, I wasted my whole allowance on that stand and didn't make a penny."

"That's true. Not all companies make money. That's because their costs, or **expenses**, might be greater than their revenues. When a company loses money, the owners, or shareholders, **risk** losing the money they put in, or invested in, the company."

"Stock owners," Mom continued, "can make or lose money just as companies make or lose money. Since no one knows for sure how much money a company will make in the future, the stock price changes all the time. People who think a company will do better in the future are willing to buy stock at a higher price. Their buying makes the price of a share go up. There are other people who think a company will make less, and they're willing to sell shares in that company. Their selling makes the price of the shares go down."

"I get it," Nathan said excitedly. "Why not just invest in companies that are making lots of money?"

"That's a bright thought," Mom said. "If we knew which companies were going to make a lot of money in the future, that would make a lot of sense. Sometimes, however, we're not so sure. Remember that *SpaceAge Video* game you made me buy you last year? Last week, you were calling it 'Dinosaur City' because it now seems so outdated. Come to think of it, I just read that the company that makes the toy, **Fast Buck Incorporated**, had to close down since no one wanted SpageAge Video in any galaxy."

"Mom, that's ancient history."

"But some companies manage to stay current year after year." She smiled. "Didn't you tell me you wanted a new bike for your birthday? Well, I have an idea. Let's buy some stock in the ***Safety Is Our Middle Name Bike Company***. I had a bike from them when I was growing up. So did your older sister, and now you will, too. I think they will be around for a long, long time."

Nathan shrugged. "So you say."

"Not only do I say, but I like the idea so much I'm going to buy some shares, or stock, in the Safety Is Our Middle Name Bike Company tomorrow."

"Where are you going to buy them, at the bike shop?"

"No, we're going to buy the shares at the stock market. Get up early Nathan, 'cause Mom is gonna trade!"

The next morning the whole family—Nathan, his dad, mom, older sister Rita, and baby Harold—were up early for breakfast.

"Are you proud of me, Mom?" Nathan asked with a big smile. "I'm all dressed and ready to go to the stock market with you."

"You look very nice dear," Mom assured him. "But we're going to the stock market with a telephone. All I have to do is call my stockbroker, tell him what I want to buy, and then he'll place my order. What your dad does is place his orders on the computer over the internet.

"Before I call my broker," Mom said, "I want to read some **research reports** on the Safety is Our Middle Name Bike Company. Research reports are written by stock **analysts** who give their opinion on the value of different stocks. Here's one report that says Safety Bike is worth $100 million in the stock market."

Nathan let out a little whistle. "That's a lot of money!"

"These analysts note that Safety Bike has issued, or sold, 10 million shares to investors over the years," Mom said. "That figure is known as the number of **shares outstanding.** Since investors are paying $10 per share today, the **market value** of the company is now $100 million. That's the amount of money required to buy up all 10 million shares of Safety Bike.

"But here's why I really want to buy these shares, Nathan. The analyst thinks that based on Safety's Bike's plans for expansion, the company will make enough money to be worth $200 million, or double its current value. That means if I buy stock at $10 per share, someone in the future might buy it from me for $20 per share, as long as the company grows according to plan."

Nathan was puzzled. "How does this guy know for sure?"

"Actually, he doesn't," Mom said. "There's always risk in the stock market, Nathan. Today all the investors in the market are signaling that Safety Bike is worth $10 a share. If business doesn't go well for Safety Bike, the price will most likely go down.

"But I never take only one viewpoint, Nathan. I've read a number of reports, and the other day, I even went down to the bike shop myself to ask them how Safety Bike is doing this year. From all these sources, I've found good indications about this company and its stock. So, I'm going to take a **calculated risk** and invest some money in this company, $1,000, to be precise."

Nathan listened as Mom called her **broker**, Steven Rich of Make-You-Money Investments. "Hi Steve, it's Sue Johnson. How are you doing? Let's make some money today. Can you tell me what price shares of Safety Bike are selling for today? 10 1/4? Hmm, it's 25 cents higher than yesterday's close of $10. Okay, buy me 100 shares of Safety Bike at the market price. I just bought 100 shares at 10 1/4, or $1,025 total. Thanks, Go! Stock! Go!"

"There, that's all there is to it," Mom said as she hung up the phone. "I'm the proud owner of 100 shares of the Safety is Our Middle Name Bike Company. I now owe my broker $1,025 and he has to place 100 shares of Safety Bike in my stock account."

"Mom, slow down," Nathan exclaimed. "What happened there? How did you know how much to pay for the stock? I thought you said it was worth $10 per share, not $10.25 per share."

"Stocks are changing value all the time, Nathan. Since my favorite analyst wrote that report, people have started buying Safety Bike. There was no one willing to sell the stock to me at $10 per share. The best price someone was willing to **offer** the stock to me was at $10.25. I found out this price from my broker. You can also find it out on the computer, via the internet. The broker saw that other shareholders were willing to sell their shares of Safety Bike for $10.25 per share. I decided to buy those same shares. The person who sold those

100 shares has to surrender the shares to his broker in exchange for my $1,025. Get it?"

Nathan understood, but did not fully trust the process. "Well, yeah, but why don't you buy those shares directly from the person who wanted to sell them?"

"It would be hard for me to find them. Our stock brokers are expected to communicate our desire—to other buyers and sellers—about who wants to buy and who wants to sell shares at particular prices. When people start buying a stock, they communicate their willingness to pay more for those shares. And for those wishing to sell a stock, they communicate their willingness to sell shares at a particular price. When these two sides match up, we get a **market price** and a stock sale."

Nathan asked, "Do you actually get to hold that stock in your hand?"

"If I want," Mom said. "The broker will send me a certificate, originally issued by an agent of Safety Bike, specifying how many shares I own. Most people these days, however, let their brokers keep their shares for them. I receive an account statement every month that summarizes how many shares I hold of a particular company. The statement also shows me how much cash I have on hand with my broker. In addition, I get charged a fee each time I buy or sell stock, so that's listed on the statement, too."

Out of the blue, Nathan's sister Rita, who was usually more interested in high school and her Russian teacher, joined the discussion. "You're all a bunch of capitalists. All you talk about is money. Why don't you talk about something important, like keeping the environment clean?"

Dad saw his opportunity to cross the generation gap. "Rita, how would you like to use your **capital**, or money, to become part owner of a company dedicated to cleaning up waste from dirty, smelly corporations? I know of a company called the ***Green and Pure Cleanup Corporation***. As an owner, you'll even be asked to vote on important decisions made by the company."

Rita was interested. "Now that's important. I could go for that."

"Good," Mom said. "I have an idea for the whole family. Let's build a collection, or **portfolio**, of stocks selected by each member of the family. We'll call it the ***Johnson Family Portfolio***. Let's put some money—or stock—together for this new family venture. If we all make good stock selections, we can use the profits to go on a nice family vacation."

"I'll put in 100 shares of the Future Is Now Internet Company," Dad offered. "It's now worth $10 a share. Your mother can put in her 100 shares of Safety Bike purchased at $10.25 a share."

Nathan volunteered, "I have $800 saved up from mowing lawns and babysitting. Let's invest that money in the market."

Rita revealed that she had $1,200 saved up to give to worthy causes dedicated to saving the earth and its environment. She said she wanted to put half of it, or $600, in the Green and Pure Cleanup Corporation.

Dad went to the computer and discovered the stock for Green and Pure was now selling at exactly $12 a share. "Should we place an order to buy, Rita? It's your money to invest." He grinned. "I must warn you, the reports I read indicate that they make a profit."

Rita readily agreed. "Let's buy it. But I do know how to shop for a bargain, you know. I don't want to pay more than $11.50 a share."

"We'll give the broker exactly those instructions," Dad said. "Let's place an order on my computer, stating that we're willing to buy 50 shares at a ***limit price*** of no more than $11.50 a share. Now, there's no guarantee we can buy the shares for less. We hope some buyers willing to pay $12 a share go away, and that sellers willing to sell for $11.50 per share appear. The broker will let us know if that occurs. Or we could even watch the stock all day on the computer to see how the market price changes." He punched a button on the computer. "There, the order is placed and now we wait."

Fifteen minutes later, Dad received a report on his computer: *You bought 50 shares of Green and Pure for $11.50 per share.* "Hey, Rita, you're now a capitalist. Your capital just bought 50 shares of the Green and Pure Cleanup Corporation. Good luck with your investment!"

Rita tried to conceal her first bit of capitalist glee, though she couldn't help but grin. "I'll show you. I can make money, influence my company, *and* do my part in saving the planet."

The Johnson Family Portfolio

"Okay, Nathan," Mom said. "Now it's your turn. What company do you like?"

Nathan thought for a moment. "How about buying stock in my favorite television network? I spend all day watching it anyway, and so do all my friends. Let's buy some shares in *Kid TV*. I have about $800 saved up from my lawn business."

Mom typed the name in the computer and found information. "Nathan, Kid TV is not a *public company*. Its shares are not traded on the stock exchange. It's a *private company* that has never sold its shares on the stock market. But I did find out the company is wholly owned by the *Really Big TV Network Corporation*. If Kid TV makes money, Really Big TV will keep all the profits. And Really Big TV Network does have publicly traded shares. They're now selling at $8 a share. Do you want us to buy some?"

"Okay. I'm good at math," Nathan said. "Buy 100 shares of Really Big TV at $8 per share."

"I can see from the brokerage company that Really Big TV is very highly ranked by many stock analysts. However, it's never good to put all your money in one company," Mom said with caution. "Something could go wrong and you could lose all your investment money."

"Then buy 50 shares of Really Big TV at $8 per share. That comes out to $400, and we can save the rest for later, like Rita did," Nathan said. He was already speaking like a natural young market investor.

Mom tapped the keyboard. "Done. The order is in. And I just got a report. Nathan, you're now the owner of 50 shares in Really Big TV. Congratulations."

"Thanks. Now, as an owner, I think I'm going to watch my television company. Cool."

The Johnsons had now constructed a ***stock investment portfolio***:

Company Name	Number of Shares	Purchase Price per Share	Latest Market Price per Share	Current Value
Future Is Now Internet Co.	100	$10.00	$10.00	$1,000
Safety Bike Co.	100	$10.25	$10.25	$1,025
Pure Cleanup Co.	50	$11.50	$11.50	$575
Really Big TV Co.	50	$8.00	$8.00	$400
Rita's Extra Cash				$625
Nathan's Extra Cash				$400

Total Value of Johnson Family Portfolio				$4,025

Every week the family checked the latest price for each of their shares on the internet, or from other news publications. As the prices changed, so did the value of their entire investment portfolio.

One month later, the value of the family's portfolio had increased by $925, an increase of 23%. Not bad. Not bad at all!

Company Name	Number of Shares	Purchase Price per Share	Latest Market Price per Share	Current Value
Future Is Now Internet Co.	100	$10.00	$20.00	$2,000
Safety Bike Co.	100	$10.25	$9.00	$900
Pure Cleanup Co.	50	$11.50	$11.50	$575
Really Big TV Co.	50	$8.00	$9.00	$450
Rita's Extra Cash				$625
Nathan's Extra Cash				$400

Total Value of Johnson Family Portfolio				$4,950

Another month later, Nathan had exciting news to share after returning home from school. "Hey, Mom, Dad, guess what? We're not the only ones investing in the stock market. Billy Snodgrass told me that his father has made a fortune 'playing' the market. He said that the Future Is Now Internet Company has made his dad a mega millionaire."

"That's right," Dad piped in. "I ran into Leonard Snodgrass at the club. He couldn't stop bragging about the Future Is Now Company. The stock has doubled in the last month. He put all his money in at $10 per share. Now it's selling at $20 a share. He said the stock is going to the moon."

Rita, who'd discovered her latent capitalist tendencies, reported from the computer. "Correction. It's now selling at $25 a share. Up $5 in one day!"

"Darn it," cried Dad. "I knew I should have put more money into that company. I could kick myself."

Always reasonable, Mom spoke up. "Hold on, Mr. Speculator. What goes up can also come down. I just heard on the **stock market channel** that the Future Is Now Internet Company would have to sign up the entire population of the globe to justify their current market value, or **market capitalization**. In the market view, the stock should be trading at $10 per share—not $25. I think we should sell our shares now and take the money while the money is good. After all, we paid $10 a share for this company only a short time ago. It makes sense to sell when the price gets too high. **Buy low, sell high**—that's what my investment club motto has always been."

Dad agreed. The Johnson family decided to sell all 100 shares of the Future Is Now Internet Company for $25 a share. For the sale, they received $2,500 in their account in exchange for their shares.

Dad locked in a profit. He bought 100 shares of Future Is Now at $10 per share, or $1,000 total. He sold 100 shares at $25 per share or $2,500. The family portfolio made $1,500 dollars.

After updating the current prices for all of their stocks and cash on hand held with the broker, the Johnsons reviewed their new portfolio value.

Company Name	Number of Shares	Purchase Price per Share	Latest Market Price per Share	Current Value
Safety Bike Co.	100	$10.25	$8.00	$800
Pure Cleanup Co.	50	$11.50	$11.50	$575
Really Big TV Co.	50	$8.00	$10.00	$500
Rita's Extra Cash				$625
Nathan's Extra Cash				$400
Cash from sale of 100 Shares of Future Is Now at $25/Share				$2,500

Total Value of Johnson Family Portfolio				$5,400

By the end of the day, the Future Is Now had increased to $30 per share. Dad was still muttering about how he should have bought more shares and not sold any at all.

Mom was more level-headed about the matter and insisted they should be happy with the profit they'd made.

Then, Nathan noticed a delivery truck bringing new stereo equipment to the Snodgrass house. Mr. Snodgrass could not have looked happier.

Nathan realized capitalism sure brought out a lot of emotions.

About a week later, the Johnsons were watching the stock market channel and heard exciting news from their favorite financial news reporter, Dudley Bullmarket. They trusted most everything Dudley had to say.

Dudley announced, "The Future Is Now Internet Company just released a statement which says, 'During the current quarter, the company definitely did not *go to the moon*'. In fact, we missed all analyst targets. While our future business is still promising, we will be suffering over the short term due to inflated expectations from the marketplace.'"

Dudley added, "Once the stock market opens, trading is likely to be heavy on the downside."

Finishing his briefing, Dudley said, "In other news, the Green and Pure Waste Company secured a huge contract to clean up the ice pack in Siberia. This stock should open significantly higher."

And sure enough, the Future Is Now shares began to trade at $15 per share. That was a $15 drop from yesterday's previous closing price of $30. No buyers **bid** for the stock at the previous day's level.

Fifteen minutes later, the stock price was still falling. The stock was now trading at $7 per share—indicating a major panic among share owners and traders in the stock market. By the end of the day the share price of the Future Is Now had crashed to $4 a share. It seemed everyone wanted to sell shares in the Future Is Now, and no one wanted to buy.

Everyone, that is, except Nathan, "Hey, I was reading about the Future Is Now. It's not like they are going out of business. In fact, I just read in one report that they might be bought by a larger company for $10 a share one day. I think it's time to buy this company when no one else wants it. After all, I'm in it for the long term. *Buy low, sell high,* right, Mom?"

Mom calmly affirmed his idea. "Let's buy 100 shares of Future Is Now at a **price limit** of $4 per share. That will use up the $400 extra cash you have on hand in our portfolio."

After a short discussion, the family agreed to go ahead with the purchase.

That afternoon, as Nathan entered the prices of the family's shares in the portfolio folder he kept by the television, he couldn't help but notice the 'For Sale' sign that went up at the Snodgrass home across the street.

"It looks like the Snodgrass family *bet* more than they could lose," Dad said. "They took too much *risk* in the market. They speculated by placing too much of their portfolio in one stock."

It was sad, but it was a lesson Nathan would never forget.

Rita also learned to enjoy the profit of her conviction. Pure and Green closed up 50% for the day, at $18 per share. Not bad. Not bad at all.

Company Name	Number of Shares	Purchase Price per Share	Latest Market Price per Share	Current Value
Safety Bike Co.	100	$10.25	$9.00	$900
Pure Cleanup Co.	50	$11.50	$18.00	$900
Really Big TV Co.	50	$8.00	$10.00	$500
Future Is Now Internet	100	$4.00	$4.00	$400
Rita's Extra Cash				$625
Dad's Extra Cash from Stock Sale				$2,500
Total Value of Johnson Family Portfolio				$5,825

Over the next several months, the family lost some interest in following the daily movement of the stock market. Stock prices were not moving much. In fact, the family portfolio seemed to be going a little backwards.

Company Name	Number of Shares	Purchase Price per Share	Latest Market Price per Share	Current Value
Safety Bike Co.	100	$10.25	$5.00	$500
Pure Cleanup Co.	50	$11.50	$16.00	$800
Really Big TV Co.	50	$8.00	$6.00	$300
Future Is Now Internet	100	$4.00	$3.00	$300
Rita's Extra Cash				$625
Dad's Extra Cash from Stock Sale				$2,500
Total Value of Johnson Family Portfolio				$5,025

Nathan said, "Mom, Dad, I don't understand the point of the stock market if we aren't making any money."

Rita piped up. "Maybe it serves us right for being capitalist pigs."

"Here's how it works, kids," Mom said, sharing her experience. "The economy has slowed down, which means people aren't buying as many goods and services. Some companies grew too fast, and then had to reduce their purchases. Some companies even fired some of their employees. When people get scared, they lessen their spending. That can hurt the profits of companies over the next few months, including the ones we own. That's why people aren't buying as many stock shares right now."

Dad unfurled a big chart he'd cut out of the newspaper. "This graph shows how the growth in stock prices has grown with the profits of corporations over time." Prices of stocks have clearly doubled, tripled, and even more than quintupled over many decades. "We're just in a temporary slowdown. The best investors stay the course and hold shares in their favorite companies. It's called **long-term investing**. Always remember that our stocks are pieces of companies we know and respect. If they make money over the long term, so should we."

"If anything is for sure," Rita chimed in, "corporations will continue to make money in the future. *Viva la profits!*"

Dad looked surprised. "Rita, I never thought you'd say such a thing!"

"Hey, we're talking about money here," Rita said with a smile.

"Viva la profits," said Harold, who was just two years old.

"Hey, maybe he feels left out," Rita said. "Let's take $400 from Dad's contribution to the portfolio and buy some stock for Harold."

Mom, who had expected this development in her littlest one, was already prepared. "Let's buy shares in the *Little Guys and Gals Diaper Company*. No matter how slow the economy is, that's one thing parents of babies will always buy. The shares are trading at $8 per share, and they've been as high as $15 earlier this year. According to my research, the company has never had a year without profits. I think it could be a good time to buy."

"Viva la profits," Harold chirped again. They all decided to buy the smallest family member 50 shares in a diaper company for $8 a share. More than anyone else, little Harold was investing for the long term. Good for him. Good for his bank account.

Company Name	Number of Shares	Purchase Price per Share	Latest Market Price per Share	Current Value
Safety Bike Co.	100	$10.25	$9.00	$900
Pure Cleanup Co.	50	$11.50	$19.00	$850
Really Big TV Co.	50	$8.00	$9.00	$450
Future Is Now Internet	100	$4.00	$17.00	$1,700
Little Diaper Co	50	$8.00	$8.00	$400
Rita's Extra Cash				$625
Dad's Extra Cash				$2,100
Total Value of Johnson Family Portfolio				$7,025

Through the years, the family made it a weekly ritual to update prices in the family portfolio. The portfolio had significantly grown in value over time. A lot of value was created. And, as one might even say, family values grew as well.

It was now time to enjoy the fruits of their labor. So, with a click of a keystroke, the family decided to sell its 100 shares in the Future Is Now at $17 per share, for $1,700 in cash.

With the proceeds in hand, it was time to go to Mega Beach Resorts, thanks to the Johnson Family portfolio. A vacation in which no one, not even little Harold, would discuss the stock market. While the family played, the stocks continued to work for their owners. There was plenty of time for the stock market when the family returned home.

As the car pulled out of the driveway, the last that could be seen was their license plate which read, "Go Stock Go".

Let's Talk Stock!

For Bigger Kids

&

Curious Adults

When a company needs money to expand its business—to build factories, buy supplies, pay workers, advertise products, or a host of other activities—it needs to turn to investors outside of the company to finance its growth.

One popular choice for companies is to sell a piece, or share, to the public. For an agreed price, usually determined with the help of an investment bank, a company will sell a set number of shares to the public in exchange for money from the new public shareholders. This event, of selling shares to the public for the first time, is known as an **_Initial Public Offering_**, or **_IPO_**. A shareholder owns a share, or part, of a company.

A shareholder owns a share, or part, of a company.

Once a company has issued shares to the public, the original buyers can sell their shares to any other investor at the stock market. The shares might go up, or down, from the **_Initial Offering Price_**, depending on how the company's business performs over time and the reaction of investors who buy or sell shares of the company.

A shareholder becomes a part owner of a business. This partial ownership entitles a shareholder to a portion of the wealth created by the company. Ownership also exposes the shareholder to the risk of losing his or her investment should the company perform poorly.

As a part owner, a shareholder has a right to vote on major decisions of the company. The more shares owned, the more votes given to a shareholder. If a shareholder, or a group of shareholders, controls more than half of all shares issued by the corporation, they can usually control all major decisions of the company.

What is the difference between stocks and bonds?

By owning a share of stock, a stockholder becomes part owner of that company. He is entitled to a portion of that company's wealth after the company has paid all its debts and obligations. The stockholder is also given the right to vote on key decisions facing the company. The more shares owned, the greater the portion of wealth and voting power given to that owner.

A bond is considered debt of the company. When a company borrows money to finance its operations, it can issue debt to bondholders. These bondholders are given an interest payment in return for lending money to the corporation. Bonds are usually issued for a certain amount of time and must be paid back in full at their maturity, or expiration date.

Many investors prefer to allocate a portion of their portfolio to bonds, as they can count on a set interest payment delivered on a regular basis, usually every six months. In addition, the original investment, or principle, is not usually at risk. The company is obligated to return this amount first, before stockholders can lay claim to the net worth of a corporation.

Bondholders are considered lenders to a corporation. They usually receive a set interest payment and the right to be paid off before owners of the company if the company should face financial difficulty. They're usually willing to accept a lower rate of return in exchange for greater security, knowing that they will be paid back in the future. Bondholders have limited upside. They will not receive more than the value of set interest payments, plus the return of the capital they originally lent to the corporation.

Stockholders are considered owners of a corporation. If a company does well, then the owner will lay claim to the accumulated profits of a corporation. Since a company can become more valuable over time, the upside is not limited. Value will grow as the company prospers. Since a company might also fail, the owner assumes risk that the company will have no profits to distribute. Therefore, a shareholder can expect higher returns when business is good, but also assumes higher risk than a bondholder when business is bad.

Bondholders will generally be paid off in full (with interest payments and return of capital) before stock owners receive dividends or money for their ownership share if the company should be sold to another company or liquidated for its assets and valuables. Creditors, or bondholders, would be paid back first, before shareholders.

As investors become older and come to depend on their investments to support them in retirement, a greater portion of bonds is often recommended. While the upside is not as great, the security of set interest payments and the return of investment capital is of great value.

Younger investors, or those who do not need to use their investments for many years, often allocate more investment capital to stock shares. These investors, with a longer time horizon, can weather the ups and downs of the stock market more easily than older investors. While the ups and downs might be more dramatic, the prices of their stocks should increase over the long term as long as they have chosen profitable, growing companies.

Learn the following and you'll sound like a stock market pro.

Both ***Market Capitalization*** and the ***Price Earnings Ratio*** are two phrases you'll hear a lot when following stocks. You can look them up in the newspaper, or on the internet. Understanding how these figures are calculated will help you better understand discussions about stocks.

Market Capitalization

The total market value, or market capitalization, of a company can be calculated easily with information found in a company's financial reports, on financial internet websites, or from the financial section of most large newspapers.

- Find out the total number of shares the company has issued or sold to investors. This figure is known as ***shares outstanding***.

- Look up the current price of the company's stock.

- Multiply the two figures together to calculate the total ***market capitalization***, or market value, of the company.

Market Capitalization = Number of Shares
Outstanding for Company

x Price per Share

Market capitalization reflects the total value of the company in the collective opinion of stock market investors. The market value implies the price a company would cost if it were sold, in its entirety, to another company or investor.

Market value changes all the time with the constant changes in the prices of stocks in the stock market.

The price earnings ratio (the "P/E" ratio)

Step 1. Calculate ***Earnings per Share***

- Find out the total number of shares the company has issued to investors. This figure, as before, is known as *shares outstanding*

- Look up the total ***earnings*** of the company over the past 12 months in the newspaper or on the internet.

- Divide total *earnings* by the number of *shares outstanding* to calculate *Earnings per Share.*

Earnings per Share   =   Earnings of Company
(for past 12 months)

÷   Number of Shares Outstanding for Company

Step 2. Calculate ***Price/Earnings Ratio***

- Next, look up the current *price per share* of the company's stock

- Divide *Price per Share* by *Earnings per Share* to calculate the *Price/Earnings Ratio*

Price/Earnings Ratio   =   Price per Share

÷   Earnings per Share

The market value of a company is determined by investors in the stock market. If buyers bid up the price of a stock, the market value of a company rises.

Sometimes, investors look at the growth rate of a company's earnings. Here's one example: If the ABC Company earned $1 per share over the past 12 months and is expected to earn $1.20 next year, it would imply a growth rate of 20% per year. If investors bid ABC stock up to $20 per share, the stock would be trading at a Price Earnings Ratio (P/E Ratio) of 20.

One rule of thumb suggests that a stock should trade at a P/E Ratio the same as its growth rate in profits. In the stock market, however, there are no rules for price. Investors, or speculators, may bid up a stock to an extremely high P/E Ratio. Conversely, they may sell a stock to a very low P/E Ratio if the company and its stock fall out of favor with investors.

In the above example, if the ABC Company earns $1 per year per share and stock traders bid the market price up to $40 per share, that would imply a P/E Ratio of 40. Some would consider that price expensive for ABC shares given the lower company growth rate. The contrast between the P/E Ratio and the company's slower growth rate in earnings might be seen as an opportunity to sell shares in ABC.

If ABC shares were trading at a price of $10 per share, the company's stock would be trading at a P/E Ratio of 10. Since this ratio is well below the company's growth rate in profits, some would consider the price low and might assess the situation as an opportunity to buy.

The P/E Ratio is only one factor. A good investor will examine many opinions, pro and con, regarding a stock before investing money into the shares of any company.

A stock market is where buyers and sellers of stock come together to exchange shares of stock for money, and vice versa. Successful stock markets create methods for exchanging information quickly between buyers and sellers. Vital information broadcast includes how much money each buyer is willing to pay for shares of stock in a particular company. At the same time, sellers communicate the price at which they're willing to sell shares to potential buyers. When a match is made between buyer and seller, a trade is made. The stock exchange insists that buyers pay for their shares within three days. Sellers must surrender their shares within three days as well.

The New York Stock Exchange, the nation's oldest stock market, lists the shares of many of the largest companies in America. It's located on Wall Street in New York City. Buyers and sellers convey information through their stock brokers who maintain membership at the New York Stock Exchange. A market facilitator is assigned to each stock at the exchange. He or she always matches the highest bidder (a potential buyer) with the lowest offer (a potential seller).

As example, at any moment, there might be several buyers expressing interest in purchasing the shares of the I.M. Big Corporation.

Bidder #1: Wishes to Buy **1,000** Shares at **$35.50** per Share
Bidder #2: Wishes to Buy   **500** Shares at **$35.25** per Share
Bidder #3: Wishes to Buy   **100** Shares at **$35.00** per Share

Seller #1:   Wishes to Sell **1,000** Shares at **$35.50** per Share
Seller #2:   Wishes to Sell   **300** Shares at **$35.75** per Share
Seller #3:   Wishes to Sell   **500** Shares at **$36.00** per Share

The market maker can match the buyer who is bidding $35.50 per share and the seller who is willing to offer 1000 shares at $35.50 per share.

After this transaction is complete, the highest price a buyer is willing to pay is now $35.25 per share. This price is known as the ***inside bid***. The lowest price a seller is willing to now sell a share is $35.75 per share. This price is known as the inside offer, or ***inside ask***.

No trades will occur until either the buyer or seller change their prices to meet the other. Or, an entirely new buyer or seller might appear to convey a new bid or offer. Suppose a new seller appears and says, "Okay, I am now willing to sell 500 shares at $35.25 per share." A transaction would instantly occur and the process would repeat all day long until the stock market closes, at 4:00 p.m. in New York.

This process is so quick and the difference between bid and ask is so small that many buyers and sellers tell their brokers that they want to buy or sell a stock ***at the market price***. Their transaction will be instantly executed at the inside bid (for sellers) or at the inside ask (for buyers).

The latest transaction price, where an owner buys shares, and where a former owner sells shares, is known as the ***market price***.

As more buyers appear who are willing to pay more for a stock, the price will go up. As more sellers appear who are willing to sell stock at lesser prices, the price of a stock will go down. The stock market, after all, is a true marketplace.

The Johnson Family Portfolio

What is the Dow Jones Industrial Average?
What is the S&P 500?

There are thousands of companies that have their shares traded at the stock market. Stock indices (the plural of index) such as the Dow Jones Industrial Average and the S&P 500 measure the stock performance of leading companies in the United States.

The Dow Jones Company has selected 30 top American companies to be included in the Dow Jones Industrial Average. In their opinion, these companies represent a good sampling of the leading companies in the United States. If the prices of shares for these companies go up, the Dow Jones Industrial Average will rise as well. The performance of the **Dow 30** is one of the most widely reported market statistics by all news organizations. This average has been around so long that it offers a good comparison to show how much the value of leading companies has grown over the years. Also, many investors consider the performance of these large companies to be a leading indicator of performance for the whole stock market.

Standard and Poors, known as the S&P, has selected a larger group of 500 leading companies. They also try to balance these companies across many different types of industries. Their most widely cited index is the **S&P 500**. Many investors feel this index represents the best measure of the overall performance of the stock market. Investment managers often compare themselves, and their stock picks, against this average. If you or your stock manager has a stock portfolio that beats the S&P 500, many on Wall Street will consider that you're doing a good job with your investment picks.

The Dow Jones Industrial Average

S & P 500

Stock prices rise when investors believe that a company is undervalued. Stock prices decrease when investors believe that a company is overvalued. The price of a stock is a direct indication of how much the market believes an entire company is worth to investors.

When a company sells stock to investors, it sells them shares in the company. The total number of shares issued by a company to investors, or co-owners, is known as the **total number of shares outstanding**. If a company has issued 10 million shares to the market and these shares trade on the stock market at $10 per share, the implication is that investors now value the company at $100 million (10 million shares x $10 per share = $100 million).

The price of a company's stock can tell you how much a company is valued by the investment community. The total number of shares issued by a company multiplied by its stock price will give you the total value of the company, known as its **market capitalization.** Investors implicitly calculate the value of a company each time stock shares are sold.

Since opinions change all the time, stock prices also change, as do the values of all companies trading shares on the stock exchange.

Stock markets do not go up in a straight line; that is, they sometimes fall. And sometimes, they fall sharply. Such a situation can be very painful for you as an investor, especially if you've started investing just prior to a fall.

The best thing to do is to keep a long-term perspective. Generally speaking, stocks rise over time with the increase in profits of the companies that trade on the stock exchange. If you have a portfolio of healthy growing companies, your portfolio should grow over time with these companies.

Many investors like to buy extra stocks when the market has these temporary downturns, or **corrections**, as they are called. It can sometimes take days, weeks, months, or even years for stocks to return to higher levels. But, if you liked a company at a higher price, then you might like to buy its shares when they go "on sale" during these market corrections. Some investors feel they can take advantage of other investors' panic by buying shares when they are cheaper.

Investing in stocks should be for the long term, for needs more than five years from now. If you'll need cash within the next year or two, then you shouldn't risk those funds in the stock market. Many short term investors have been forced to "sell low" when the market experienced a downturn and they hadn't kept adequate cash in the bank for their daily needs.

Historically, stocks in the United States have grown at an average of more than 11% per year. That's a higher rate of return than most people can expect from leaving money in the bank, or even under the mattress. For the long term, few investments can beat the performance of the stock market.

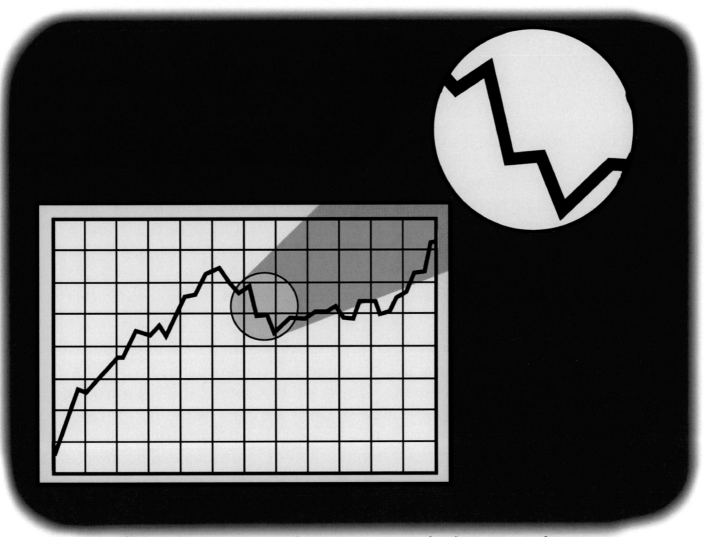

These downturns can be scary...over the long term they
are short blips in a rising stock market.

Growth Investors purchase shares in the stock of companies with fast-growing profits. The strategy is based on the theory that companies with fast and growing profits will be followed by robust prices in the stock market. Does this strategy always work?

Not always. While it's true that a company with ever-increasing profits will increase the value of the company for investors, sometimes investors in the market bid up the price of a company's stock to unsustainable levels. The higher the price of a stock climbs, the higher the risk that it can fall when something goes wrong with the company. And remember, sometimes yesterday's star companies can become tomorrow's dud companies. So investing in companies with fast-growing profits—and high-flying stock prices—is a form of **growth investing** that sometimes carries great risk.

There are many companies that are not appreciated by investors in the stock market. They might have temporary problems. They might have businesses that are stagnant. However, the total value of all of the company's holdings (the value of its cash in the bank, property, factories, etc.) could be worth much more than its current value in the stock market. Stocks in these companies are known as **value stocks**.

Furthermore, if the entire stock market were to fall during a stock market correction (a period in which all or most stocks fall, often after a period of bad news for the nation and its economy), then the prices of value stocks tend to fall less dramatically since they were already lower to begin with.

Investors who focus on such relatively **undervalued shares** are known as **value investors** and are happy to buy shares in undervalued companies. While the companies they invest in are ignored by the market in the short term, these value investors are confident that eventually the value of their companies will be recognized.

Value investing is usually best for the patient investor.

A combination of growth and value investing should be used in composing your stock portfolio.

INVESTMENT DIVERSIFICATION

PORTFOLIO

PORTFOLIO

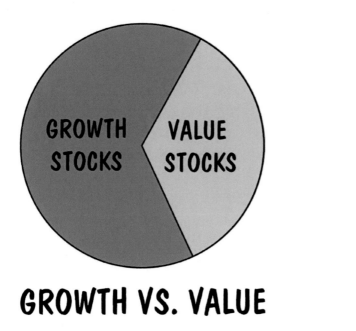

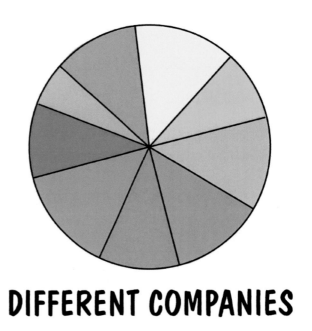

GROWTH VS. VALUE

DIFFERENT COMPANIES

When investors put their money into the shares of a favorite company, they have an opportunity for high return. If investors buy stock at $10 per share and the value of the stock rises to $20 per share, investors would double their investment.

However, what happens if a company reports bad news to investors? Sometimes, companies that look strong prove to be solid disappointments. In the worst case, a company could lose much or all of its value in the stock market. For investors who invested all or most of their savings into one company, the loss could be devastating. Not only could this knock an investor out of the investing "game," it could also tie up an investor's money in a losing or stagnant company when the rest of the stock market might be surging ahead.

The best way for investors to lower this **_company risk_**, as it is known, is to diversify their holdings across many different companies. That way, the failure of any one company cannot hurt the overall wealth of an investor.

For example, suppose an investor has a portfolio (or collection) of 10 stocks with an equal $1,000 in each stock. If one company totally failed, the price of its shares might approach zero. The investor would therefore lose $1,000 out of a total portfolio of $10,000. This loss would hurt, but it wouldn't devastate the investor's entire savings. In fact, the other nine stocks in this case might even perform well enough to make up for losses of any losers within a portfolio.

What is a mutual fund?

A ***mutual fund*** is an investment company that invests its capital in the stocks of other companies. Investors buy shares in a mutual fund company. The manager of the mutual fund then invests that money in the shares of other companies. Some mutual funds own shares in hundreds and hundreds of other companies. If the value of these companies increases on the stock market, then the value of the mutual fund should increase as well.

Mutual Funds
(List of Stocks Owned)

Auto	Hi-Tech	Utilities	Restaurants
General Motors	IBM	Texas Utilities	McDonald's
Toyota	Microsoft	So Cal Edison	Starbuck's
Daimler-Chrysler	Cisco Systems		Lone Star

Investors in mutual fund shares, in effect, are investors in many different companies. Mutual funds can hold stocks or bonds in different industries as well. Mutual funds can provide instant diversification for an investor.

Many investors like the convenience of mutual funds because they don't have to choose individual companies for investment. The job of selecting a portfolio, or collection, of stocks becomes the job of the mutual fund manager.

By investing in a mutual fund, an investor can diversify his or her portfolio. Instead of risking all his or her money in one, or only a few companies (remember, some companies do lose money), a mutual fund investor has money spread across a large portfolio of companies owned by the mutual fund. It's unlikely that all companies owned by a mutual fund will lose all of their value.

Mutual funds must be selected carefully. Some managers are better than others, and their funds might have specific goals. There are funds focused on hi-tech companies, and others are focused on companies in foreign countries. Some funds buy shares in large companies, while others acquire shares in small companies.

Researching a mutual fund for investment is as important as investigating an individual company for your stock portfolio.

A small amount of money invested when you're young will grow to a large amount of money by the time you're an adult. Look at the following example.

Let's say you're 15 years old and invest $1,000. If it can grow at 15% a year, your investment will be worth $4,046 in just 10 years.

This is known as **compound growth**. Not only does the original investment earn money over time, any gains on the original investment can be reinvested as well. If you start with a small amount and leave all or most of your investment earnings in your investment account, you can hope to grow your investment portfolio even faster.

Compounding is so powerful that a person starting an investment plan later in life will have great difficulty in catching up with your wealth.

Take the example of a 50-year-old man who starts investing later in life. Even if he puts away $1,000 a year for 15 years, he will still be behind the investor who put away $1,000—once—when that investor was 15 years old.

That's not to say it's never too late to start. It just makes it harder to catch up when you start later.

So enjoy your youth, but you'll do yourself a great favor by saving some money for investment while you're young.

Do The Math!

Amount Invested	Age	Growing at 10% per Year	Growing at 15% per Year
$1,000 Once	15	$1,000	$1,000
After 1 Year	16	$1,100	$1,150
After 5 Years	20	$1,610	$2,011
After 10 Years	25	$2,593	$4,046
After 20 Years	35	$6,728	$16,367
After 30 Years	45	$17,449	$66,212
After 40 Years	55	$45,259	$267,854
After 50 Years	65	$117,391	$1,083,657

versus

Amount Invested	Age	Growing at 10% per Year	Growing at 15% per Year
$1,000 Every Year	50	$1,000	$1,000
After 1 Year	51	$2,100	$2,150
After 5 Years	55	$7,716	$8,754
After 10 Years	60	$18,531	$24,349
After 15 Years	65	$35,950	$55,717

Many people claim to be broke. They say they would save if only they had a little extra money.

And yet, those same people always find ways to pay for food, clothes, a new car, entertainment, or whatever is really important to them. After buying everything they really want, there's no money left to save.

Try it the other way around. Decide how much you want to save each month from your allowance, babysitting service, or part-time jobs. Before spending money on anything else, first put away at least 10% of your money into a savings account.

You'll be surprised how quickly your savings can add up to a lot of money, even enough to begin investing in the stocks of your favorite companies.

Remember, when you save money, it doesn't go away. It's there for you to use in the future. And while your money is invested, it's working for you. It grows over time. In the future, you can buy a whole lot more than those who choose not to save at all.

You can bank on it!

Little Harold shall
inherit the Earth!

The Author's Story

Behind Go! Stock! Go!

Go! Stock! Go! has been a work-in-progress for many years.

I had often wondered why the basics of investment math weren't covered in high school or in most college courses. While only requiring knowledge of grade school mathematics, the subject was reserved for those taking higher level studies in business education.

Most investors, if they learned investment terms at all, did so over a long period of trial and error, without ever fully understanding the subject.

For many, the stock market became a casino, with investors risking their hard-earned dollars on stock tips and hunches. They lacked the necessary tools to objectively compare the stocks of different companies.

Stocks should be analyzed against a standard set of measures. Purchasing shares in profitable companies should be investments, rather than uneducated bets.

Investment books are invariably written in a taxing academic style. Worse yet, books written for young people often talk down to them.

Go! Stock! Go! is for readers of all ages. The picture book format is fun and informative and will be a cherished reference book.

Though designed with children in mind, the book is also written for adults. Storybook pictures are easy-to-follow examples and just as friendly to adults as they are to children.

While working as an investment professional, I originally wrote *Go! Stock! Go!* for family and friends.

This early version remains largely unchanged. Home computer trading methods were already the norm for many stock investors. Today, it's easy for young investors to research stocks and companies with search-engines and financial websites. Mature investors might still prefer traditional sources such as *Barron's* or *The Wall Street Journal*. Information is widely available, so this choice is left up to the reader.

This book is designed to make commonly used investment terms understandable and easily calculable.

The mathematics of investing are often intimidating on the surface, but usually revisit grade school lessons with cartoons to help readers visualize concepts that might otherwise be lost with text alone.

Therefore, the original concept, humor, and dialogue of *Go! Stock! Go!* also included a complete set of drawings, situations, and dialogues that have been carried forward into the current edition.

A talented young artist named Adam Wolfson added character and a unique investor personality to each member of the Johnson family.

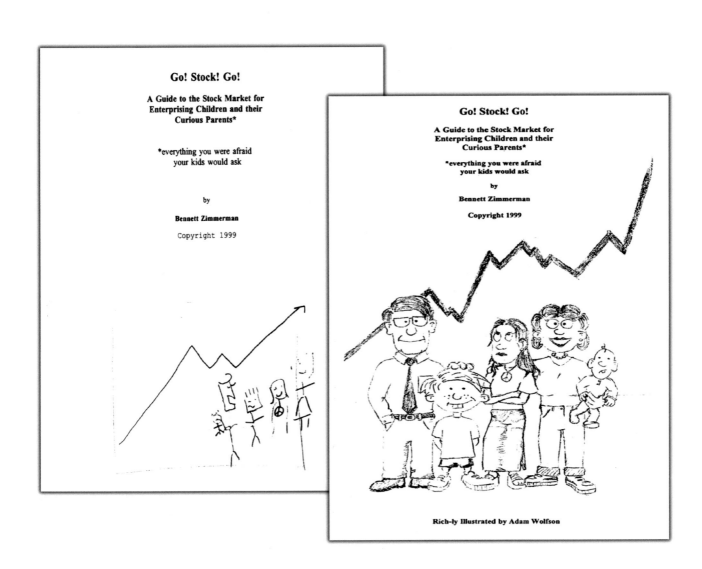

Kathy Kamel, a professional artist, brought vivid color and life to the original conceptual drawings designed to illustrate sometimes abstract concepts to readers.

The section, Let's Talk Stock, was inspired by comedian Joan Rivers and her often used phrase: *Can we talk?*

While working on a later edit for this book, the media was filled with reports of her sudden passing. I had always considered her one of the great *Turnaround Artists* of our time. I like the *Way* she lived her life.

The news reporter, who becomes a part of the Johnson family's research time together, is an amalgamation of my favorite reporters. I extend particular appreciation to early CNBC anchors Ted David, Maria Bartiromo, and Joe Kernen who were my constant on-air companions.

In closer circles, Jamie Cook-Tate encouraged me to dust off and prioritize *Go! Stock! Go!* as a timeless and much-needed publication for today.

Lifelong friends Lisa Horowitz and Susan Mashiyama faithfully read the work from cover to cover, often reminding me of basic grammar rules we had learned in grade school.

I am grateful to Ginna Moran and Jan Moran for bringing *Go! Stock! Go!* to a professional level, ready for publication.

And, most of all, my gratitude to Kendra Johnson, who bears no relation to the Johnson cartoon family of the story. She often reminded me that *Go! Stock! Go!* could become a book loved by many, many readers.

And that's a good thing.

Bennett Zimmerman
Santa Monica, California
July 2015

Thank you for reading *Go! Stock! Go!* For news and updates, visit www.GoStockGoInvest.com and join the mailing list.

Let us know how you liked *Go! Stock! Go!* If you found this book helpful, please leave a review on Amazon and on Goodreads, Facebook, and other places for your fellow readers.

The FOURTH WAY WORLD, LLC
1318 Yale Street
Front Suite
Santa Monica, CA 90404

Made in the USA
Columbia, SC
27 October 2018